Free Verse Editions

Edited by Jon Thompson

Also by Joshua McKinney

Saunter

The Novice Mourner

Mad Cursive

SMALL SILLION

Joshua McKinney

Parlor Press
Anderson, South Carolina
www.parlorpress.com

Parlor Press LLC, Anderson, South Carolina, 29621

Library of Congress Cataloging-in-Publication Data on File

978-1-64317-046-6 (paperback)
978-1-64317-047-3 (PDF)
978-1-64317-048-0 (ePub)

1 2 3 4 5

Cover design by David Blakesley
Cover image by Raymond Meeks. Used by permission.

Parlor Press, LLC is an independent publisher of scholarly and
trade titles in print and multimedia formats. This book is available
in paperback and ebook formats from Parlor Press on the World
Wide Web at http://www.parlorpress.com or through online and
brick-and-mortar bookstores. For submission information or to
find out about Parlor Press publications, write to Parlor Press,
3015 Brackenberry Drive, Anderson, South Carolina, 29621, or
email editor@parlorpress.com.

for my students

Contents

Contents

Small Sillion

Selion, n. *A furrow turned over by the plough.* nonce-use.
　　　　　　　　　—Oxford English Dictionary

No wonder of it: shéer plód makes plough down sillion / *Shine.*
　　　　　　　　　—Gerard Manley Hopkins

To say: I have lost the consolation of faith
though not the ambition to worship,

to stand where the crossing happens.
　　　　　　　　　—Forrest Gander

First

Hum

When I smelled green through the blur
where its wings were, felt
the whir of their arc, heard the red
of its ruby throat-scales, tasted the dart of its forked tongue
afloat in the foxglove—my only desire was
to tell you.

My weed-work stopped. Hands
in earth, I knelt by the garden wall,
and suddenly that world seemed remote.

I called to you, aloud, and the words I spoke
were rote, broken, each one an arbitrary token
of the tiny bird that came to kiss the flowers.

It was then I knew my exile's full extent.
The phenomenon of pungent sound is brighter—
sheer iridescent now there then—
than the hours of thought without flesh. Once, to be
at one meant to act, so I have tried to make this
matter.

Point of Reference

Thou

While I stood there, bewildered,
I must have looked a long time
back to that other world,
which held the best of me—

the pasture with its broken tractor,
an old roan who loved sugar,
a brother dead before birth,
the summer cool of a storm cellar,

its rich odor of dirt. I don't remember
much before the forms changed,
before the pungent colors chimed
to charm the wary creatures forth.

Eyes shining, they led me here
unharmed. Earth's common light
was strewn about; my eyes were strewn
with weeping, also with flowers.

Down in the River

bottom, I went walking at dawn,
                through the thought-out grass to
      where the last rabbit track failed
          among dredge tailings, looming
like cairns around me. That brumous
      landscape destroyed all compass,

and I stopped, cloaked in the cold fog,
             listening. Off to my right, a dog
      barked, distant, practicing
          its old partisan art : something joyful,
something doleful as the oldest
      sound. And it seemed to drift

toward me as greeting, nearly
             tangible, but breathable, too,
      like the cloud I stood hidden in, all
          bearing lost in a cold inspiring,
vapor drawn into my body entire, sown
      in the furrows of my brain's tilth.

How long I waited I can't say.
             Then I heard the cry again, more distant
      still in that heartbroken place
          where shaken, I took a step forward,
solitary and slow, and started at a sound
      I made myself, an almost human name.

Prayer for My Daughter

The nervous, hurrying
bird ahead of us says
something that isn't kill
deer. O ear of my ear,
hear what throat-flung
comes incalculable
through bright air to bless
the continual and misspent day.
It is fair beyond my wanting
and my fear. The names for it
fail all underfoot and above.

You see its murmur
in a foreign tongue, such
strangeness as was mine
a little while, in a parking lot
where hot cars inflame
your green *why*'s softly
are keeping to shine. O eye
of my eye, see the looking
bird's inquiry even here,
and eye of my eye, shut
every window with an apple tree.

The Understanding

Each morning the scrub jay proclaims
        something I've forgotten   something
sacred   something wholly
              mundane.

Not in his tongue does the fallacy exist
       only in my translation of it?

Perched at my desk I watch him
           outside on a live oak branch.
     Now
and then he drops to the lawn to eat a grub
       or grab an acorn which he stores
always out of sight.
               I've read that he can recall
up to two hundred caches   the type of food in each and
      its rate of decay.
            Such facts
       refracted by symbolic action   are all I have
   to know birds by.

In his sermon St. Francis accused some birds
     ("ye neither sow nor reap")
          but they   in gratitude   expressed their joy
   by motion and by sounds—
       those sweet ones
we call song—   unlike the screech
         of the scrub jay on his branch
tilting his head as he watches me
     with one dark eye   as if to say   Why
       do you not understand my speech?
And if I could bring myself to answer:

Because I cannot hear your word   you
whose lineage is land   whose element is air
foundry of your voice
                     molding all sound
to its likeness   both wondrous and strange.
          ⁓

          If all that I can understand were all there is . . .
but no   the jay is otherwise
                     a something   I cannot translate or touch.
          What won't suffice
must   and that fact draws me to my desk
                     each morning
where distracted by the racket outside
                              my understanding
                     damned
          within the limit of this language
I rejoice in its failing
                              in the mind's grateful
graceful sense of boundary—
                     the faith
that I am favored with
                     such bounty.

Near Song

The music is good and, each his own, all will make my song more pleasant. —Jaufré Rudel

I

Matinal

Imagine there is nothing
to be made up
for in the morning

"Some birds are poets"
good mentors singing
the imagination lonely

mindful freedom enduring
garden trouvaille o see
this my green author

how rapidly new
flowers   today cinquefoils
the gods are

II

Noontide

outside the office
building amid the
countless passing

lantana leaves my
daughter sees
motion   a mantis

clutching a moth
aflutter and is happy
for the mantis

minutes later our
business done and
passing back

the other way
she finds the
mantis but no moth

and is happy for
the moth. "Look
closely, that is all."

III

Dusk

From the Old English
dox, the time just before

I know more about
horses than heaven

"… a brass band
with wings on it …"

what line of force?
and if unwitnessed

what arrogance? Or in
the words of others

what unseen acre
ventured upon

a portable Everest
incriminate when

fin carved firmament
downward to flame

the vole owns the thunder
the earwig and ant

"There is poetry as soon
as we realize

we possess nothing."

IV

Vespertine

Whilhom in Sarlat
Jaufré Rudel broke
a lute string tuning and

in the hush heard
bat wings whisper fine-
boned and torchward

errant in generous measure
hence   in that company
no one   for a moment

breathed   sensing other
being beyond their circle
the very air vibrissal

they strove sounding
eyeshine absent under
a nictitating moon

Glede

All fall the oaks turn their backs
to my gradual prayer
the holy I take leaves the color of alarm.
Some day as a boy

over a field, fog-hugged and mud-baltered
my not yet body thrashes and tears
not yet in the talons of
that grey-winged hoverer

not yet. So I wait to witness witless
my true prayer. As one day
I listened alone. Maybe I did really.
As really, I hold a red leaf

squeeze a little singing nothing,
the only experience I have ever had.

Lepus

I thought I saw through the ear of a hare, where
it sat in the morning sun, light-glow
behind dilated vessels there, so near
the warmth of the ambient air,
yet below

the heart's heat at the hare's core—
and what's more, I thought I could hear the blood rush
down, into its long limbs abeyant,
aware as the nerve current sang in its flesh.

And I smelled sage
merge with stone, fresh earth-breath after pre-dawn
rain, the wet nearly gone as the sun rose
and the hare, unmoving forth in its massive stillness
leapt fierce and alone with its ear-light
through me.

To the Chief Musician

The world puts forth its crying,
        hurled into the future's morning after.
    A cold wind flays the trees.

        Leaves whirl with the crows,
their dark sayings shining
    to any ear inclined. I hear

the shards of voices, hearken
        unto a void that words believe
    yet cannot know. A notion

        of wind and leaves and crows
sutures the mind against the dimmest
    glimmer of laughter lining each day—

a token of hope
        that the flayed can turn
    a cold wind golden.

Point of Reference

Still early and dawn sows its first handfuls of light over the ridge,
kindling to gold the tussocks of bunchgrass scattered across the
scrub. The dust is down, still damp with the night's light rain, the
sage musk and petrichor so fresh and sharp he has to stop and
stretch his lungs with it, while his dog trots among the shrubs and
stones, tracing the faint missives of woodrat and hare.

He tells himself he brings her here to remind her she's a dog—a
mongrel pup his kids saved from the pound (a little setter, perhaps
some hound), and even then so beaten down she cowered at the
slightest word. His kids have gone to college now, so he brings her
here, where he remembers walking as a boy, searching for arrow-
heads with his father, the petroglyphs they chanced upon at the
base of the escarpment, the figures etched in rock by a people long
since erased, and how he felt he could almost read those shapes.
There were mustangs, too, and from the ridge he used to watch
them grazing on the plain below and name their colors—bay,
buckskin, pinto, palomino, roan—shining in the sun.

Hushed, he'd watch for hours, until some presage startled the
lead stallion and the herd would thunder off across the desert and
the sound of their hooves would rise with the dust and fade away
and then only the dust remained. Bound by so much absence, he
finds it hard to move. But what stops him now is that the dog,
always aquiver in her quest for sign, is doing something he's sure
she's never done before: she's frozen, standing stiff, right foreleg
cocked in mid-step, tail straight up, nose thrust forward, her whole
body aimed toward a juniper thicket he calculates is maybe thirty
yards ahead. It's clear she senses something there, and is by sense
compelled to adopt a posture dredged from blood, a silence and a
stillness bred to signal presence.

His eyes dart to the dog, then to the trees and back again, but
he cannot see beyond the thicket. All attention now, he scans
the silhouette of dark limbs for any sound or movement; but his
straining senses fail, fold back upon themselves. Under the weight

of his listening eyes and looking ears, his sounding breath, he feels his own inflection in the world's flesh, feels he is perceived. Charged by vague encounter, changed by what he cannot name, he stands there waiting with the dog, whose gesture he understands, in a distant sense, without knowing the nature of what it points to.

The river was

green except
where it was silver I drove
above it wondering

how could I have forgotten
its name passing
so often that way

these many years
the road unwinding
my faith in the failure

of memory
come closely upon us
as rite   now

holding your hand
easing into atonement
the other life

we led   conducting
into the doctrine
of a moment only

which will not take us
all the way O
my love my driving

eyes the river
is green
except where it is

silver
and it is silver
everywhere

A Relic

When you are gone in our bed
                   the cat takes your place
                                   beside me

where love's object is
                   lack, an eye too deep or
                                   the broken sight I swim in

lashed to sleep I dreamed you had come
                   to my senses departing
                                   in arrival the past appears

so dearly opposite the sunset
                   sky the country of the drowned
                                   the undone

outstretched whirled under
                   in waking I discover
                                   on your pillow a trout's heart

A Valentine

Lower than grass, the first yellow crocus
breaks ground under the pomegranate tree,
where amid the branches, leaf-bare
and barbed, the remnant of a last spent fruit
dangles black as a gobbet.

I, too, was homeschooled in violence;
my eyes, too, have been worsted
by the terrible immediacy of love.

I give my dog a bone; she becomes
a frantic gravedigger in the garden.
Equally excited, sure of uncertainty,
methinks there is no place like hell.

And now I see my son returning
from his run under the rain, where lower than grass,
ancient plankton rainbows the gleaming streets
and starlings herring a sky
above the earliest yellow flowers.

Perhaps we will glimpse purple tomorrow.
Little crocus, when did I forget to see again?

Dip

Only when the alphabet comes into a culture, when the phonetic alphabet arrives, only then does that culture get this odd notion that language is an exclusively human property or possession. And the rest of the land falls mute. —David Abram

The river's virtue is event:
      the dipper's temperance entwined with liquid song
          which, as occurrence, lasts
      only as long as an ear can cast
          across the living river.

Prior to writing, a man might demonstrate prudence
      by plucking a lyre, or fortitude
          by fighting. And as each situation changed,
    an act arose which one might emulate
          the way that river water "rushed" and "splashed"
and vanished in the flow of human speech.

But long ago such worldly union passed
      into ideas that only an eternity could teach;
          severed from sense, they hovered in some other
      timeless place, solid as a disembodied god.
          "Justice" became a bloodless good, a word
heard in the head, a pure abstraction beyond change.

After writing, the action on a page can only be imagined.

                        A dipper bobs
                        its body up and
                        down; it thrives
                  by diving in the flux.
                     Go to a river
                   and ask a dipper
                     what a dipper
                      does. What does
                        a dipper do?
                             It dips.

Sealm

whoso it thought
      its burst and bother

    consider some mother's came side-born
this world brought other victims
    & they would be least words to us

to many & of me
    ~
enter now leafborn   consider

    how worshiped was the serpent in the hole
the wolf bad as he they declared
    or it consider   or born they consider

he name forth as a such
    until the strangeness is
    ~
    invisible little wave catch what is fell
& least to touch   & half polluted
    point to those as yet by lettered forgetting

own the one unlikely
    thought across the notes

    gone beyond flowers O purpleward horizon
where we wait to call it language
    exhaust into yolk the beautiful beast of it

with ear to hear earth-
    breath will wren thee
    ~
    sung in unknowing
myself a traveler passed like rain
    a song here hoping up somewhere

the is once returned to it
    into a lost

    the lair lips the birth   peace in the limbs
of the horse in the scale of the snake
    forever savage the meaning
              ⁓

& whoso would it enter
        enter it

    be as thou & bid come
creatures themselves
        & betwixt pains dwell surely

be they hid as oft as thou
        before it were such   lord

A Mundane

Mundane n. *A dweller in the earthly world.* Obsolete.

—Oxford English Dictionary

To contemn the world and to enjoy the world are things contrary to each other. How then can we contemn the world, which we are born to enjoy? Truly there are two worlds.

—Thomas Traherne

There is another world, but it is in this one.

—Paul Élouard

Chalk

Returning from a run, I walk
the last block to cool down,
down the fractured sidewalk,
past the abandoned house,
its waist-high weeds and sodden
newspapers, down the street
past the mute windows of
my meth-addict neighbor,
the driveway Rorschached by
her new man's monster truck,
down the street beneath jets
dragging exhausted trails across
the sky, under the olive tree
which has bloodied the concrete
obscenely with its fruit.
My daughter kneels in our driveway,
chalking her brother's outline as
he lies on his back, limbs splayed,
grinning. Her shape in yellow pastel
sprawls nearby. As I approach,
she looks up, asks me to lie down.

Another Day in the Perishing Republic

That I might thrive,
I went out to run
as I had the day before
and the day before that.

It was late afternoon;
the lowering sun
hung in the pine tops,
smoldering there

as ravens roosting
loosened veils of
pollen, until the very air
shone gold. Awash in light,

I marveled at the real
world, its fullest
wonders felt, not told.
Content, I labored

up a grade to where
two ways converged,
and in the distance saw
a dancing man,

car door still open
beside him. I thought it joy,
or perhaps awe
at the same light I had seen.

He finished then, and
turning, saw me,
still far off, and raised
a hand. I waved back,

watched him as he drove
away. And all was good.
But when I reached the place
where he had been,

and stopped, and stood
there, sweating, out of breath,
I found a king snake
he had stomped to death.

Post Hoc

In the saddest cities, the farthest flung
      reaches of Rome, the wisdom was
that certain vermin sprang from waste:
      maggots from rotting meat,
frogs from marshlands' putrid fumes,
      mice from moldering husks of wheat.
Though the battlefield urged other,
      the open eyes of the dead saw too late
the truth of it. Those bodies bloating
      in the sun bespoke their loss
in the tongueless tongue of death, time-
      honored unto dust, unheeded as their armor,
whether leather, bronze, or steel, succumbed
      to weather and to rust. As a foul scent
in a gale, their soundings passed, leaving
      corruption born of no union, many
out of none, an inversion of raw
      beauty, its true cause obscured
by a sudden detonation of flies.

7th Displacement

Every day was death's anniversary. So endeth.
The neighbor's cat hit, left lying in the street.
The need to bury things before the kids get up.

Beneath the split-trunk oak where more than
once I'd seen a five-lined skink peer out
six feet down
the ground gave way and I fell to where I swam
drunk under the trees.

Though I was drowned, at last my body broke,
reduced to a skull with its flat-toothed evidence.
So endeth. The infinite instant

I could smell the pull of the root forest, anchored
in the breath the pall of earth
its throng and stack
bequeathed to the margin, all.

Animism

My daughter is talking to her toys
again. "Would you like some tea?"
she asks, pouring from an elfish pot.
First she serves the sock monkey
with a missing eye, then the polar bear,
the tiger, and the dog—all awkwardly
propped in little plastic chairs
around a little plastic table.
She serves me, too, and I pinch
the ear of a tiny china cup
between thumb and forefinger,
as from the sofa I consult the newspaper
whose daily exegesis is doom.
Above kitchen clatter my wife asks,
"What does it say?" It says
that in Italy 660,000 liters of oil
have reached the Po River. It says nothing
of purpose lurking behind the words,
of ink spilling as oil spills becoming
mundane, from *mundus*, "of the world."
My daughter tells me the monkey says
I should drink my tea. No one would
call her crazy, yet the forgotten river
gods go unappeased. I sip my tea.
Somewhere a dark ichor is oozing
through pipes onto pages that, once read,
carpet the grease-stained concrete
of my garage. It was in such a place,
on a Sunday morning years ago, I first learned
of the soul. I was no older than my daughter,
attendant to my father who lay beneath
his beloved Thunderbird, when his hand
slipped from an oil-slick wrench and
he cut his knuckles, cursed the car.

The Current

Somewhere there is always a wind somewhere
a wind is always there its thousands of
blind eyes groping for anthems

somewhere a wind carries away children's voices carry
the wind's garments lashed to their backs
across sun-cracked plains

somewhere a wind is a memory of rivers dammed
by a wind whose parentage uproots
the gaze of exiles

comes the elsewhere that is the wind is the embodiment
of turning one's face from an empty sleeve
twisting once more in a wind

and somewhere a wind presses itself once more against
a woman who can no longer feel the reason
behind such advances

there is a wind whimpering in the universe despaired of
an abandoned barn where it has smothered
its pet shame a breeze

is the lie a wind tells and tells once more erasing smoke
from gun barrels a wind fires the forest's
genuflection of broken limbs

pointing somewhere a wind cannot go to the place
our inarticulate eyes stutter at the edge of
the steep sky's order

somewhere there is always a wind rousting ghosts
from the ridge crust of mountains
is a page of old snow

dotted somewhere always somewhere else with blood
for the good of a god do not think
a hawk is free the eagle

is trapped by a wind a humble wind that refuses to be
the wind O anonymous wind somewhere always
always somewhere else

is a wind distributing agency O somewhere wind tending
the crazy waving of rent banners that were once
the truce flags of clouds

Vestige

When my wife motioned me to the picture window
and pointed to the garden where
our daughter and son sat beneath sunflowers—
the dog and both cats
sprawled around them as they toyed with dolls in the dirt,
a honeyed eastlight washing over it all—
my first thought was to save the scene.
And perhaps because I was tired
of the digital's immediacy, the ease with which
it erased my failures, or perhaps
because the moment demanded more resolution,
I ran to the hall closet and pulled down my old 35 mm
which had no film and then
ran to the kitchen drawer wherein were tossed
all things utile and useless and rummaged
among the screwdrivers and flashlights, the scissors and
tape, the twist ties and rubber bands,
for the film canister I thought I'd seen some weeks before
and sure enough
buried at the back I found it and popped the lid and
poured into my anxious palm two seeds or so I thought
for an instant before recognition claimed them
as dry buttons of blood,
the twisted tissue of the kids' umbilical remnants
my wife had told me not to save (*disgusting*, she'd said)
but which I'd kept and hidden
and then forgotten for reasons I don't understand and
then from the window my wife said *you missed it*
and even as she said this I heard the children arguing outside
and realized I could smell something foul
and that it was what I held in my hand
and that it smelled like what it was,
like flesh gone bad,   like,   like

Incredulity

Because thou hast seen me, Thomas, thou hast believed;
blessed are they who have not seen and have believed. —John 20:29

Frequently noted, Caravaggio's failure
is that of not indicating the physical sources
of his light. In *The Incredulity of St. Thomas*,
for example, three apostles draw near Christ,
peer at the wound in his side. Thomas
extends a rigid finger into the fleshy slit,
as Christ, indulgent, guides the fascinated hand.
Or does he restrain perhaps what otherwise
would probe too deeply? He seems to understand
that in their eyes he comes to them as man,
not disembodied spirit, but as flesh.

With his robes fussy as some drapery swag,
with his coiled locks and physiognomy refined,
he is without halo or symbol divine. The wound
is physical evidence of his existence in this world,
and yet no longer of it. Hence the look
on Thomas's face: is it fascination or fright?
But the light—and this was my point at starting—
the light escapes some point beyond the frame,
the master's hand uncertain of its source.
It is a minor point perhaps. The eye soon returns
to the old motif of hands, to the pale, incruent wound.
So too with Caravaggio. His models, we are told,
were musicians, whores, cardsharps—all strangers off the streets.

What came to pass in Potsdam where the masterpiece is
housed? Such a tangible phenomenon—it teases,
out of touch. You can imagine what came next:
the wide-eyed stares, the screams of disbelief.
Security rushed in with its arresting hands.
Then the threats, the epithets: "A rustic materialist

without imagination or tact . . .", how "there are laws"
to deal with such an act. "Stupid, stupid man,"
said the luminous woman standing next to me.

Harrow

The real is not
confused with truth
today my truth is
bleeding gums
sublime enough
to prove trivial
tomorrow it is
the first of
February and proof
comes without
asking a tree
frog's small flame
resonant and sound
enough to borrow
for this poem
draws attention
to itself even
as it indicates
demise

Beyond Reason

We were at the zoo. Its lie of the veldt calmed me as I peered over chain link into a pit, hyenas pacing trails in dust. A minute maybe, and when I looked up my daughter was gone, the many children all the wrong children, my body suddenly a thing of pulse and pressure—paralyzed by my desire to cry out, by my need not to. A minute maybe and then

she emerged from the ground—the tunnel of the meerkat exhibit, where kids can crawl in to witness the animals' excavations—running to tell me what she'd seen, and I, moving quickly toward her, my terror lifting like a loose balloon, and then, rushing in to take its place, emotion changing with each stride—relief, then rage.

Columbine(s)

Its blossoms, inverted,
a cluster of doves.

The hope that describing be
an act, yet after

the fact, the unbearable
entropy of description.

To speak this powerlessness,
to change the faces

that come back and back and
back again with our fatigue,

the way names blur together—
some birds become a bloom,

a bloom, a place, a place,
an event repeating its loss.

Rebereaved

The slack beginning of the year's end
tightens in the glow of fallen leaves.
Urgent lessons of smoke erase the trees
in the logic of this ashen light that bends
the day to breaking

                                      beautifully
then mends the whole

horizon
                      something to believe

     as I groom the ground

   to receive

                              an absent snow
           driven

                an absent wind

Before the Bringing Forth

The last generation thought itself the last.
Yet here we are: each year in crisis,
bought from the dead who know
our living worth too late. God, it's hot today
as I cross the vast black of the shimmering,
tar-soft parking lot, where starlings hop
between the cars. This state,
insolvent though it is, becomes me.
So much of what the earth has suffered
is fraught with birth, with an errant offer to create.
Thirty years ago I dozed under oaks here.
Deer grazed in the long grass,
and the girl I lay with blushed at their approach.
Cancer took her early, but her daughter still lives
on Maidu Street. Looking back,
I am shown myself, no first youth
reflected in a doe's eye black as asphalt.
If it could, the last generation to think itself
the last would make an earth without a past.
God, it's hot today, and I am fast awake,
finding my life a borrowed garment,
which at fifty fits me less well than in a past
that was yesterday, or years ago,
when I will take it off at last.

Evasive Behavior

As I drove down Maidu Street
this morning, a gray squirrel
crossed in front of me and

I eased off the gas, slowed
a moment as it gained the shoulder
then changed its course and

darted under my car. I felt
the small disturbance of its death
shudder through rubber and steel,

sighed at the folly of a creature
whose fear had made it go
too far. But what could I do?
I shook my head. I drove on.

In Paradise

We see these Edens in the world, believe in them.
—William Bronk

A Rendering

The roadkill opossum rots quickly
in spring, its body breaking down
along unguessed gridlines. Each day

there is more and less of it. As we pass
the spot, my dog strains at his leash,
nosing toward the stench, the bones

unfleshed, insects nearly finished
with their excavations; a thin echelon of ants
trails away into grass. I tug my animal

back from the carcass, to *my* senses
all but gone, yet to the dog still vivid
in a rich matrix empanelled on the air

for his delight, webbed vectors of creatures
passed and passing into other forms
in the language of decomposition,

which he conjugates again, fleshing out
the traces, seeing beyond annihilation
of mere light-reflecting surface. And though

I name him *beast*, or *pet*, or *friend*,
and bend him to my will, he suffers it all
meekly. In him the world is recomposed,

the roadside dead drawn in in inspiration,
their quick contours recast into a living
whole. Through his breath they walk again.

In Paradise

The perception of beauty is a moral test. —Thoreau

have you availed
yourself of spring meadows
their lush grasses green   and wild
flowers
and tarried there rolling
some large stone aside   to find
the sharp-tailed snake   *Contia tenuis* which otherwise
spends its life   in seclusion

and have you   gently
lifted one
and have you seen
its rosy dorsal hue   the sheen
of its scales   the contrasting
cream of its belly

and have you felt it   quicken
the heat of your warm-
blooded hand passing into it

and have you observed
at the end of   its tail
the sharp spine
the function of which is not fully understood

and have you looked
long into the tiny eye
a darkness without reflection

and have you smelled
the bitter scent it secretes
its sole defense   though feeble
against you

and did you release it   back
          to cool earth   to shade
beneath the stone
          and turning homeward   feel
its motion still
         in your empty hand
feel it truly   a living thing?

no?

good god man

[From the vast city / escaped into]

From the vast city
escaped into
hazard woke me

a "rather nasal, hard
querulous *ennk*"
& the rapid

rek rek rek rek rek
as the pied & blue-
black sheen

hopped aground
in the dawn
grass beneath

the olive nearing one
hundred & I
perceived all

that was ripest
what with rain &
the sun soon after

questions turn
away from my tongue
strange passages

where I dozed
but kept my body
plump with grain

over the vast city
hazard wakes me *ooAAH*
cooo coo coo much

larger than enough
was the day that began
with magpies & ended

with a dove.

A Morphology

The wind taught me that I am not a hawk
    the oak that I am not a squirrel scurries
  circles up a tree

      flames too
spiral trunk-bark toward the
        crown of smoke thick
   where the sun drowns

      dark-veiled I am
not the wind the hawk I think
     blames me for this

   is the fault of the mind the wind
      moves the smoke yet drives the fire
the moral of which is ash is

     change in form aims to be always
   never what it was its kind the same

Ophidian

Near the American River
                    yesterday I thought
          I caught sight of
a little rattle disappearing
                    in blonde grass summoned me

silent I struck into this field
                    to look careful for those
          that died unseen
where I placed my feet
                    in the falling

my kind mastered
                    before fire & the small violence
          in me coiled
against the larger violence without
                    sight of a snake

moving lovelily in the on-going grass
                    near the American River

          today I stand in the ashes
of someone's firework
                    mind full of yesterday

my legs were blonde grass.

"Come Down"

And he made haste, and came down, and received him joy-
fully. —Luke 19:6

The sycamore of the Bible is a kind of fig tree:
Ficus sycomorus. And into such a tree,
Zacchaeus climbed, to gain a truer vantage
as Christ passed. Or so the story goes.
How can we know intent after the fact?
Disparate causes may lead to the same act,
and effects grow more miraculous
each time the teller pauses. Perhaps
an earthly hunger drove his ascent,
to scrabble for fruit beyond his reach.
After all, climbing was not new to him;
a small man, Zacchaeus had proven himself
in a world of taller men. He was a chief
whose wealth increased his stature, proving
once again that providence can raise
the shrewd and dwarf the less industrious.
Why pay for figs when they were near at hand?
The Lord helps those who help themselves.
Besides, he liked to be above the press
of rubber-necking zealots on the road.
Consider how Christ must have felt
when he glanced up into the glare and saw
Zacchaeus cradled in that tree, a man who did not give
a fig for those who stood there in the dust below.
Much has been made of Christ's command,
which was by most accounts direct.
One wonders what his tone revealed.
A momentary lapse perhaps, by one who hoped
to make a point. It's likely that Zacchaeus understood
such parlance (so vital in his line of work.)
He was a man whose station could accommodate
a certain grace because his own commands were
not to be ignored. The subtleties of saving face

sometimes demand that one become a host, and so,
smiling, he saw the task at hand: to descend
and have some commerce with the man.

Forms of Refusal

In darkness, deer stare out
from this poem, their eyes
bright in the glare of my flashlight beam.

I have written myself into this
landscape, come mosquito-bitten and
groping to regard them as they are

here, hoping that the shame
I must wake to will melt in their nearness.
Wading in shadow, I approach

the names I have given them: *doe* and *buck*
and *blessèd wild thing*. Unhurried,
they bend to crop the grass in this field

beside a river. I no longer know
what I have made as they allow me to pass
voiceless among them. I tremble

as they show themselves. Now
one doe comes close, so close I look
deep into her dark eye and see a man

standing among deer in a field.
His cheeks glisten; he seems to be weeping,
yes, I hear him sob—and at the human

sound the deer in there, those tiny deer,
bound off into black. "Come back,"
the man says, and turning toward me,

imploring, he raises his face, pointing
to the sky with his eyes, which
I can see now, are blind.

A Summoning

All night from the outskirts the coyotes unfurl
their shrill counsel I have heard

the shine of their eyes
where mine can only whine anxious
into the dark
trying to remember something I cannot

remember something was it their first name
perhaps the last people to speak it
have wandered off
into a moment the moon blinked

coyotes speak of this
of everything but only once I wake

late in the dark I hear my blind ears panting
unable to follow their song
into the eyes I stopped seeing in dream

they asked me to come to them I went
wide and quiet past that place.

Flammarion

Tonight, nothing will be exemplary. The repetition
of earth's imagery, beyond all
change, is beautiful.

Armed with knowing, my son will leave soon.
I am on my knees in the backyard,
consoling the dog.

Above me, the dying light lets its three bats go
unstraightly off into the growing
static of stars.

I imagine the lie of their light shining over a jungle
I will never see. I imagine
small mammals

tonguing nectar there, gathering starlight
into the bright tapestry of their sight.
I see them only

in my mind's eye, and they can never know
with what reverence I long to behold them
truly. I am so broken.

Are they diminished unseen? A bat's black passes
blacker against the dark, is jerked away
between stars,

an oblique intercession. My vision of nothing
is my right damnation. Those times
when I am absent

in the world, full-present in the void where nothing
begs remembrance, a snake skin sloughed
in a bramble.

My ideas are wrong. However terrible it is, forgive
the world. A truce is possible, a tolerance
that has no place

in the actual world. It is why I have nearly forgotten
the time at that Eden, when I, too,
drawn by desire,

walked out into a new reality and looking aloft, saw
the matter of it: stars are flowers.
Pick any one

and say, dwindling flower, without knowing your name,
I know you, for tonight's true example is
that nothing

between me and the ghost-light of stars is a space
with no shape to occupy. And that nothing
requires our belief.

Glory

The arbor's splendid
vassalage rends the morning air.
I believe in pieces that perhaps
the only revolt is death.

Here I sit brokenhearted under the blooms.
I have coffee and a stack of student poems.
I own an iron deck chair wet with dew.

～

If I did not know
better, I would swear bird song rose
from the little Victrolas
covering the garden arch.
Their brilliance hurts
my eyes, but I know better. And what am I
to call their color? "Heavenly Blue" the seed packet said.
In Japanese, Morning Glory is *Asagao*:
asa (morning) *kao* (face),
and in her opening stanza,
a church bell ceases yet tolls the disappearance
of a girl's grandsire
who fought the tiny sword men on the islands,
who smoked bees from wooden boxes
while he smoked himself to death.

～

I arose and went to the mountain,
but the glade was silent,
the glacier gone, the meadow sere.
And round about the woods were strewn
with the pale blooms of ass-wipe, unburied
by those who also sought the wilderness.

～

Now the poem's speaker—whom one must not assume is
the author—is crying

missing the man she called "Pops" with his bees
and his Bull Durham

telling how his bee boxes have fallen "into disrepair,"
almost hidden in the "grass like green hair"

leaning like abandoned barns
in the field near the apple orchard where the crop grows
smaller every year.
~
Now is the augury of late migration,
of empty hives, of early pupae
twitching in the brackish pool
behind my neighbor's foreclosed home.
~
There is a man I would like to know
better, a man who trekked in sun-dry deserts
with a backpack full of poems,
tracing the sinusoidal track of *Crotalus*
in the graven silence of sand.

He still writes letters in beautiful script
on lovely paper, and in a letter I did not write
I told him of the night I knelt
to fuel my Stihl in the dank soil of a fire line,
told him how I watched the terrible and ravenous light
crawl down the ridge, told how
I saw old growth in flame immured, charred
trunks horrent upon the horizon's bare convex. Told how
I thought it intimation of the end.
~
Her trouble (as I've told her) is telling:

She remembers his tenderness
when she tastes honey from a plastic bear

how no sweetness can compare
to what he'd spread on bread for her at lunchtime

with calloused hands she loved to hold.
And how she misses the bees

that like her granddad won't come back.
⁓

A mercury-risen day, and now I see
the tiny trumpets have withered,
their blue apertures twisted shut,
and from the kitchen window my son asks,
      If tuna is contaminated
          with mercury,
          what happens
        if you microwave
      a tuna sandwich . . .

      Does it explode?
⁓

My son, have you considered how
     you will live in a world
         without tigers?

And have you seen any bees lately? O
    vigorous disappearances

lifeafterlifeafterlifeafterlifeafter
⁓

Out of nowhere
now here in the poem
the girl has grown,
and now the poem
in the girl has grown,
and now the girl in

the poem has grown
in me and now

under pretence of teaching
I must write something
in response. Dissembled and furthering,

the shadow of my hand
veers dark and mutant over the page:

Will you learn
to live without? or
Will you know better? or
Please, do not close your morning face? or
perhaps, (though I know better)

Dear Student, named for a flower,
how I love this terrible poem
about your grandfather's bees.

Inspecting a Patch of Grass in the Backyard, I Delight in My Senses, Get Distracted by Thought, Then Delight in My Senses Again

bright coupling of
air and bird
                song drowned in
      the drone of jet

engines Doppler off
over red petals
                paling against
      fence boards

where the heard
assemblage confounds
                the word
      camellia is

picked in what passes
for attention to
                detail but
      how might the smallest

shard read
read outside
                our grammar
      of default?

to question such
thinking I hold still
                the smell of dog
      in my hand

the near instance
of this where
                    senses consult
        the will

which wills while apart
a part of
                    the will fights
        the willing I

outside myself
an ant takes a stand
                    on the edge of
        a fact called clover

Perishing Ode

Because I have come to this
field of flowers, our coupling becomes
me, a stranger to prayer. And

when I consider you, Death,
and how I took you for a foe
before my breath was deep

in the intervals between,
every innocence becomes thunder.
I shut my eyes and look

as the sun falls. In someone's book,
sheep are tearing wolves;
but in mine, written only once,

there is neither sleep nor waking.
Amiable thing, I glimpsed you twice
across the vast expanse

of my parents' passing. I wonder
now: Which senses can I keep?
Perhaps this blind mouth,

its silent call, with which here,
in the kitchenette of a flax blossom,
I interrogate your musical name.

Spelt

I am hearing the shape of a sunbeam and believe it
is like the dead smiling in their grief
completely light
is the spring at which they drink
called forth from the waiting of things.

From above every miracle is a storm.
I am come here with this life
on my body, that I may accept earth : look
up and see a whyless sky : hear
the wounded eachness of thrushsong
in a blessed stand of wheat and more silence.

A sunbeam's like the dead regard their roses
completely light
still living or wished without.
Their wild engines all bend becauseless.
I believe in an ocean of pale hands
waving so dark on a first morning
that something thought of a sunbeam and more silence.

Late Testimony

The mountain makes itself seen,
its looking back a mode of speech.
I took my body with me there,

and each stone, each tree within
my sight's reach hid itself in me,
making its voice visible.

Then I felt myself ready
to rejoice at what I had not heard,
to see the flowers redolent of red,

their silence, whose color is
slightly always a cacophony
the eye approaches, eager, seeing

and seen, a thing unspoken,
caught in the expanse between
the waking eye and the broken

book, which opens up and takes
them all unlooking down
from the mountain within me.

Heir

The open field entrusts itself
to me—and to you,
its sole enjoyer. As one is shown

alone to be the world's end,
its whole unfolding
growth attends a strange felicity.

My infant is a toddling saint.
He knows only
to laugh at what he seems to control,

running among starlings, lifting his hands
to make them fly.
He believes that what has flown

alights anew. It's what the grass,
what the sunshine, says.
Happily deposed, the body continues

its history, toddles to a close,
the last to learn. I think
that's what I meant by being born.

Aspect

This forenoon it rained, and
as an April shower should,
relieved the outrage of the land.

For a time I stood, an actual man,
at ease and of no sect, siding
with no power against good,
inclined toward an empty hand.

Alone, there seemed reason
enough for peace. How suddenly
after all I loved well. Upon this mountain
I stood amid flowers and stones,
until I could stand no more.

A breeze arose. The sky cleared.
My windward eye asquint,
I saw sunlight kindling cities to the east.

Small Sillion

in the meantime the earthworm's tender
                    overthrow unperceived
          in the ground I strode on whose surface
      sensitive to touch reflects
the eye's mute logic the invisible
      shape of smells
                excreted castings—
          the gizzard-worked grit-
scoured ochre scored over
      the cheeks of men
                themselves become loam

we shall

          each creature

      inside the soul
          of our own flesh

plough a small sillion

          free

                & freely perceived

Last

Unselved

For is the tree of the field a man, that it should be besieged by you? —Deuteronomy 20:19

The silence of a place where there were once trees
        is a question
                still in the tongues of leaves

and I have heard the wind-poured
                hymn that dwells vacantly
in the idea of a house with its radiant furniture
        the whole white world to come

deep in the dream groves
        whose quelled citizens abandoned oak
                rowan where the sun sank red-
        berried in forgotten shades
the watched voices of birds are asking

        in the living room of a beauty been
        which is a world of wounds
                which was death's green exalting
        before some saint stepped
    out of the linden out
        of the ash

Notes

"Down in the River" – The title of this poem is borrowed from the American folk song "When I Went Down in the River to Pray," sometimes called "When I Went Down to the River to Pray."

"Near Song" – This poem contains quotations from John Cage, Charles Ives, Erik Satie, and Henry David Thoreau.

"Glede" – Any of several birds of prey, especially a European kite (*Milvus milvus*).

"*Lepus*" – Latin word for hare.

"A Valentine" – According to legend, Valentinus was a jailed doctor and Christian priest who sent the blind daughter of his jailer a crocus. The flower's healing powers brought her sight, and her first vision was the flower and Valentinus's note, "From your Valentine."

"*Sealm*" – Old English word for psalm.

"*Post Hoc*" – I am indebted to Donald Revell for the phrase "detonation of flies," which is adapted from a line in his poem "The Lesson of the Classics."

"Animism" – On February 24, 2010, the Po River in Italy was contaminated by an oil spill coming from a refinery in Villasanta through the Lambro. It was estimated that the spill was in the neighborhood of 600,000 liters.

"'Come Down'" – I am indebted to Keith Waldrop, whose poem "The Master of the Providence Crucifixion," was a catalyst for this poem and contains the botanical information cited in its opening lines.

Acknowledgments

Grateful acknowledgment is due to the editors in whose publications these poems first appeared:

Alehouse Review: "Beyond Reason"
The Antioch Review: "Glory"
Boulevard: "Hum"
Colorado Review: "Animism," "Aspect," "In Paradise," "The river was," "A Relic," "The Current," "Small Sillion," "Thou," "Lepus," "Inspecting a Patch of Grass in the Backyard, I Delight in My Senses, Get Distracted by Thought, Then Delight in My Senses Again," "Unselved"
Denver Quarterly: "[From the vast city / escaped into]," "Ophidian"
diode: "Flammarion," "A Summoning"
Fire and Rain: Ecopoetry of California: "Point of Reference"
Free Verse: "The Understanding," "To the Chief Musician," "sealm"
Interim: "Harrow"
Late Peaches: Poems by Sacramento Poets: "Down in the River"
Marsh Hawk Review: "Before the Bringing Forth," "A Rendering"
Mixer: "Perishing Ode"
Notre Dame Review: "'Come Down'"
[PANK] Magazine: "Near Song"
Parthenon West Review: "A Valentine," "Glede"
Phantom Drift: "Forms of Refusal"
River Styx: "Post Hoc"
Subtropics: "Vespertine"
Turnrow: "Incredulity"
Water-Stone: "Another Day in the Perishing Republic"
VOLT: "Spelt," "Prayer for My Daughter," "A Morphology"
ZYZZYVA: "Chalk"

The author wishes to thank the following poets who have helped shape this book: Matthew Cooperman, Peter Grandbois, Brenda Hillman, Tim Kahl, Susan Kelly-DeWitt, Donald Revell, Beth Spencer, and Randy White.

About the Author

Joshua McKinney is the author of three previous books of poetry: *Mad Cursive* (Wordcraft of Oregon, 2012), *The Novice Mourner* (Bear Star Press, 2005), and *Saunter* (University of Georgia, 2002). He is a recipient of the Dorothy Brunsman Poetry Prize, the Dickinson Prize, the Pavement Saw Chapbook Prize, and a Gertrude Stein Award for Innovative Writing. He is coeditor of the online ecopoetry zine, *Clade Song*, and teaches at California State University Sacramento.

Photo of the author by Anita Scharf.
Used by permission.

Free Verse Editions

Edited by Jon Thompson

Overyellow, by Nicolas Pesquès, translated by Cole Swensen
Physis by Nicolas Pesquès, translated by Cole Swensen
Pilgrimly by Siobhán Scarry
Poems from above the Hill & Selected Work by Ashur Etwebi, translated
　　by Brenda Hillman & Diallah Haidar
The Prison Poems by Miguel Hernández, translated by Michael Smith
Puppet Wardrobe by Daniel Tiffany
Quarry by Carolyn Guinzio
remanence by Boyer Rickel
Rumor by Elizabeth Robinson
Settlers by F. Daniel Rzicznek
Signs Following by Ger Killeen
Small Sillion by Joshua McKinney
Split the Crow by Sarah Sousa
Spine by Carolyn Guinzio
Spool by Matthew Cooperman
Summoned by Guillevic, translated by Monique Chefdor &
　　Stella Harvey
Sunshine Wound by L. S. Klatt
System and Population by Christopher Sindt
These Beautiful Limits by Thomas Lisk
They Who Saw the Deep by Geraldine Monk
The Thinking Eye by Jennifer Atkinson
This History That Just Happened by Hannah Craig
An Unchanging Blue: Selected Poems 1962–1975 by Rolf Dieter
　　Brinkmann, translated by Mark Terrill
Under the Quick by Molly Bendall
Verge by Morgan Lucas Schuldt
The Wash by Adam Clay
We'll See by Georges Godeau, translated by Kathleen McGookey
What Stillness Illuminated by Yermiyahu Ahron Taub
Winter Journey [Viaggio d'inverno] by Attilio Bertolucci, translated by
　　Nicholas Benson
Wonder Rooms by Allison Funk

90